Art on the Road

Art on the Road
PAINTED VEHICLES OF THE AMERICAS

by Moira F. Harris

with photographs by Leo J. Harris

Cover drawings by David J. Bell.

ISBN 0-9617767-1-4.

First edition 5 4 3 2 1

Library of Congress Catalog Card Number 87-62244.

Design: Nancy Leeper

Produced by Stanton Publication Services, Inc., Minneapolis

Printed and bound in Japan by Dai Nippon

Photograph appearing on page 13 is by courtesy of Fred Ward Productions, Inc.; on page 32 is by courtesy of the Museo de Arte Contemporaneo, Panama City, Panama; on page 46 by Cathy Holmberg; on pages 80 and 81 by M. K. John; on page 100 by Dicken Castro and on pages 85, 86, 94, 98, 99 and 101 by Camilo Moreno. All other photographs are by Leo J. Harris.

This book is dedicated to
John T. Flanagan who went with us to Costa Rica
and Panama, and to
Cathy and Mike Holmberg who helped us to explore
Haiti. Thank you for sharing the trips as we all
discovered Art on the Road.

Contents

Foreword

Once on a London visit I hailed a taxi near Portobello Road. To my surprise as we headed towards Hyde Park it became almost a triumphal procession; my taxi and its driver were greeted repeatedly by other drivers who honked and waved as we passed. What made it easy for other drivers to recognize this taxi was its coat of bright red paint, passsing like a cardinal through a flock of somber crows on the London streets. This book deals with other vehicles whose coats of paint make them stand out on the streets and highways of the Americas. Although painted vehicles could be studied on a world-wide basis I have limited the focus to the Americas and some of the unique examples found there. Among others, the colorful jeepneys of the Philippines, the decorated Afghan and Pakistani trucks, the mammy wagons of Ghana, and the painted ox carts of Italy all deserve recognition, but are beyond the geographical limitations established for this book. The ox carts of Costa Rica, the buses of Panama, the Tap-Taps of Haiti, the chivas of Colombia and the kustom cars of the United States all express through their decoration the tastes of owners and artists, illustrating aspects of popular culture of their times and places.

Although some of these forms of transportation are older than the twentieth century, the history of decorating them is not. Painting on ox carts began about the turn of this century in Costa Rica, while the decoration of the chivas, buses, Tap-Taps and cars came about much later, mostly after the Second World War. In each of the chapters of this book, the history of a particular painted vehicle is discussed and illustrated. Research and photography for all of the chapters were completed in 1987, unless otherwise noted.

The ox cart, bus, chiva and Tap-Tap are all privately owned vehicles of commerce. Their decoration is intended to signal them out, to set them apart and thus advertise their services. They are intended to be unique works of art whose decoration will be admired and remembered. The painting is thus selected by the owners, unlike the unsolicited graffiti names which cover the subway cars of New York. Their decoration is usually the work of specialists who suggest subject and style to the owners who commission the work. The kustom cars are privately owned collector's treasures. They, too, may be decorated by specialists, while the transformation of chassis and engine and the installation of interior creature comforts are the labors of love of their owners.

Like the contemporary outdoor murals to which they are often compared, the decoration on these painted vehicles will not last forever. Ox cart, bus, chiva, Tap-Tap and car will be exposed to the whims of weather, traffic exhaust and other pollution and the scrapes and scratches of accidents. Paint will need to be refreshed and repaired frequently, for a shabby, poorly decorated vehicle wins neither riders nor prizes. Again, like the outdoor mural, the subjects and designs on these vehicles reflect developments in popular culture. Television, movies, popular music and cartoons all offer images which have been used on painted vehicles. Religious subject matter is frequently chosen and political topics are just as strenuously avoided. For those who view them, painted vehicles provide a glimpse of ever changing popular taste and a truly mobile Art on the Road.

Moira F. Harris
St. Paul, Minnesota
October 1, 1987

1 - The Ox Carts of Costa Rica

About the year 1800 plants of the Coffee arabica strain were brought to Costa Rica from Cuba. Climate, elevation and soil were thought to be suitable for coffee-growing there and this proved to be abundantly true. The hilly terrain of Alajuela and Heredia provinces provided ideal growing conditions for the crop. Coffee soon became Costa Rica's major export, as it has been ever since.

The major problem with raising coffee in the highlands of the country was the poor or virtually non-existent road system. This caused great difficulty in delivering the beans to market at Puntarenas, Costa Rica's principal port in the nineteenth century. Ox carts, introduced from Nicaragua, quickly became the most appropriate form of transportation. Long after major roads were built making other types of vehicles usable, the ox cart has remained in favor on farms and rural roads.

In the twentieth century the painted ox cart became a symbol of Costa Rican history and folklore. It was used as a subject by Costa Rican writers, poets and painters. Motifs derived from ox cart design were used on everything from clothing to store fronts, bus shelters and garbage cans. Craftsmen continue to make and paint ox carts in the traditional sizes, but they also create numerous variations from miniature toys to bar carts. Even the ox cart wheel has taken on a separate life of its own as a house decoration and entrance marker in much the same way that wagon wheels function in the United States.

"La carreta de bueyes" (Spanish for ox cart) is a two wheeled wooden vehicle. Cedar or guanacaste wood is usually used for the wheels with yellow alligator wood chosen for the cargo box. The cargo is placed in the boxed area above the axle. Sometimes only poles are needed to guard items being transported, but more often the cargo is enclosed with panels which, incidentally, can be painted. A tongue is linked to the yoke which is fastened to the horns of the oxen. Early ox carts used wheels made of a solid cut of wood between 1¼ and 2½ inches thick. Later, when fewer large trees were available, cart makers began using a wheel formed of 16 pie shaped wedges held in place by a narrow rim of metal. The metal machinery used to squeeze the wedges into position, the rim and other metal axle parts were all originally imported, but later came to be manufactured in Costa Rica.

Ox carts were probably first built by the farmers themselves when they felt that farmwork justified the use of a vehicle and the expense of

Ox cart, driver and
friends, in a 1965 urban
setting. Copyright Fred
Ward Productions, Inc.

Measuring coffee beans in 1928 on the finca of Guillermo Wille, in the Canton of Acosta. An ox cart waits for the load in the background. Photographed by Manuel Gomez Miralles, an early Costa Rican photographer.

Garbage can in Sarchi decorated with ox cart motifs.

Entrance to the
Alfaro ox cart factory
in Sarchi, with gate
posts painted in
oxcart style.

Metal rims for ox
cart wheels, waiting
to be completed at
the Alfaro ox cart
factory.

oxen. Gradually, specialized ox cart factories (fabricas) were established in towns near the coffee growing region. Old reports mention Puriscal, Escazu, Cartago and San Jose among the former locations of ox cart factories. In 1987 fabricas remain only in Puriscal and Sarchi. Those of Sarchi are the best known because of concerted efforts to include the town on tourist itineraries.

During the nineteenth century ox carts were a constant sight on Costa Rican roads carrying sugar cane and other cargo, but especially coffee, to the Pacific coast port of Puntarenas. In 1860 Anthony Trollope was amazed at the steady stream of ox carts he witnessed:

> "But during the morning and evening hours the strings of these bullock carts was incessant. They travel from four till ten, then rest till three or four, and again proceed for four or five hours in the cool of the evening. They are all laden with coffee, and the idea they give is, that

Wooden wedges at the
Alfaro factory, waiting to
be inserted into the metal
wheel rims.

the growth of that article in Costa Rica must be much more than sufficient to supply the whole world. For miles and miles we met them, almost without any interval. Coffee, coffee, coffee; coffee, coffee, coffee! It is grown in large quantities, I believe, only in the high lands of San Jose; and all that is exported is sent down to Punta-arenas, though by travelling this route it must either pass across the isthmus railway at a vast cost, or be carried round the Horn. At present half goes one way and half the other. But not a grain is carried direct to the Atlantic." (Trollope, 1860: 267-8).

Frederick Boyle, who visited Costa Rica a few years later, commented that the road from Puntarenas to San Jose was lovely with its border of palm, palmetto and bamboo trees. The traffic of the ox carts was so great that:

"...at every hundred yards a great tree has been left to divide the currents, and the rope-like lianas hang down from the branches, and wave crimson blossoms in the traveller's face. The thick bamboos are cut and tended roughly, that their crooked thorns may not obstruct the pathway." (Boyle, 1868: 206).

Ink line drawing by F. Millon Gonzales of an ox cart loaded with sugar cane.

In addition to being numerous, ox carts made a distinctive sound as they rolled ponderously along. John Lloyd Stephens described the sound he heard on the road to Alajuela in 1841:

"They [the wheels] were made of a cut, about ten or twelve inches thick, from the trunk of a Guanacaste tree, with a hole in the centre, which played upon the axle almost ad libitum, and made the most mournful noise that can be conceived. The body was constructed of sugarcane; it was about four feet high, and drawn by oxen fastened by the horns instead of the neck." (Stephens, 1841: 350).

What Stephens considered a mournful noise was heard by others differently. Carlos Chaverri of Sarchi described it as "trac-a-trac", a sound which he said varied for each cart. Farmers' wives were accustomed to listen for the distinctive sound of their husbands' carts and thus for them it became a welcome sound of return. A cart whose wheels were quiet would not announce an arrival and would not be considered a well-made cart at all.

Of course the musical sound of one ox cart could become a cacophony when the steady stream of ox carts was en route to port or market. Enrique Vargas, a San Jose lawyer, recalls that ox carts were once forbidden from entering San Jose at night lest they keep the sleeping citizens awake. Ox carts and their drivers were obliged to stop at the outskirts of town, resuming their journeys in the morning when the "trac-a-trac" sound of their wheels would not be so disturbing.

Workers, oxen and carts removing sand from a river. This 1926 photograph was also taken by Manuel Gomez Mirralles.

A family goes by ox cart
to a fiesta at San Isidro
del Cardenal in this 1920
photograph by Gomez
Mirralles.

The musical sound results from the "play" between the axle and wheel. The fit of the moving parts and the quality of the wood contribute to the musicality. As Lascaris and Malavassi observe in their book," La Carreta Costariccense", the most musical carts are not always the most durable, which is certainly not the first time an aesthetic decision has outweighed a practical choice.

Ox carts have always been primarily working vehicles. They were used to carry crops to market and for military transportation. The cart was used early on, for example, in the military campaign of 1856 against the filibusteros of William Walker. But carts were used for festive occasions as well. Carlos Chaverri suggests that this use of carts led eventually to their being painted. On saints' days and other holidays when gifts were to be brought to the church a farmer would decorate his cart with flowers, as is still the custom in Costa Rica as well as in Spain, Portugal and Italy. Flowers in the cart, on the cart and on the horns of the oxen made such an attractive picture that the idea grew that carts should have a more permanent decoration in paint.

Although ox carts were painted in many Costa Rican towns it was apparently a Sarchi man who first thought of painting the wheels of a cart that he had built. The Chaverri fabrica had existed in Sarchi since the 1880's, but it was only about 1900 that Don Fructuoso Chaverri painted a four pointed star in blue and white on a red background on the wheels of a cart. The painting was done on a solid wheel of cedar. Later, Don Fructuoso began building the sixteen wedge wheels whose sections could inspire a more complex pattern of points and geometric shapes.

The design on the wheels continues to be based on the points of the star as Don Fructuoso first designed it. The points of the star or the rays

An early Chaverri wheel fabricated from solid cedar wood.

Another early Chaverri wheel, fabricated from sixteen triangular wedges of wood.

are now so elaborated that they appear to have layers with curvilinear forms interspersed. Carlos Chaverri suggested that this trend began from watching the optical illusion created when the wheel turned. The points seemed to multiply and expand as the wheel revolved.

On the sides of the typical cart each panel is a separate composition. A man who had worked for the Chaverri fabrica early in his career, Don Urias Cespedes, stated in a 1971 interview that the side panel paintings were his invention. First he had painted the corners of each panel and then developed a composition that filled the entire space. (Quoted in Lascaris and Malavassi, 1985: 76).

In a chronology quoted in the Lascaris-Malavassi book, the Chaverris gave 1915 as the period when the four color designs began and the earliest time for the painting of flowers on the side panels. By 1930 hearts were being included in the designs and five years later small flowers with stems in Venetian style were introduced.

Dark tones in the Spanish style were painted on carts about 1940, while by 1950 interlaces were introduced. (Ibid. 56-7). Background colors have changed as well. Don Carlos Balser of San Jose stated that a gray green was the typical color for backgrounds in the 1920's, as a side panel in the collection of his daughter indicates. Today orange is often used as it seems not only cheerful but durable. Painting is done freehand and without the use of patterns, but fabricas often keep some examples of older work so that customers have an idea of possible designs from which to choose.

Motifs painted on carts from Sarchi are curvilinear and geometric yet are never intended to be representational or naturalistic. Those from Puriscal are said to include birds or geese in their

Series of ox cart wheels and drawing, showing the development of layered points, floral elements and border designs. The wheels were photographed at the Chaverri factory while the drawing was photographed at the Cooperativa in Sarchi.

Rays were arranged to follow the lines of the wedges, sometimes with a border and sometimes allowing the design to fill the entire space of the wheel.

Don Carlos Chaverri
poses with an ox cart
prominently displayed at
the Sarchi factory.

Side panel of the cargo box and the yoke of an early ox cart, displayed at the Chaverri factory.

Two side panels painted at the Chaverri factory, dating from around 1900 and 1925, respectively. From the collection of Ana Maria Balser de Alvarado of San Jose.

Worker in the Chaverri factory with ox cart wheels as inspiration on the background wall.

An old ox cart wheel displayed outside the Chaverri factory in Sarchi.

Ox cart makers sign their work as this side panel from the Alfaro factory demonstrates.

The Alfaro brothers display portions of an ox cart in progress of construction (cargo box and yoke) at their Sarchi factory.

designs. At one time it was believed that the town and fabrica could easily be determined by looking at the style of painting of the carretas.

Certain conventions remain in the painting of ox carts. The wheels have a design based on the original four pointed star; the panels have symmetrical compositions of curvilinear forms which resemble textile designs of the Renaissance. On the slats which rise above the cargo box the design incorporates an elongated "S" shape. The same shape is also seen on the tongue. The yoke is painted with curvilinear forms centered above the heads of the oxen.

To date, no one has suggested an exact source for the designs found on ox carts. Unlike so much of contemporary folk art in the Americas there is no link between ox cart design and Costa Rican PreColumbian art. The motifs chosen are clearly part of European decorative traditions, but whether the original sources were textiles, ceramics or wood carving is, as yet, undetermined.

Cart painting can take one person about five days to complete. At the Chaverri fabrica the building of the cart may be done by apprentices while the painting is the job of specialists. Ox carts are made in many sizes, from table top toys to a miniature size designed for serving cocktails.

The Chaverri factory makes ox carts in many sizes, from toy to full size. Painters are kept busy reproducing the patterns on wheels of varying dimensions.

The Costa Rican ox cart, as a national symbol, is reproduced on this 1970 postage stamp.

The retail price of a completed cart in 1987 is about $500. Both the Alfaro and Chaverri fabricas estimate that they complete about 30-40 carts per year. Forty years ago, Carlos Chaverri said, they were building almost one cart per day. In the heyday of the painted carts it was important for a successful farmer to have a new cart every year and he would sometimes pay just a bit more to have his painting handled with special care.

Every year oxen are blessed on the feast days when other animals are blessed. That is obviously a moment for carts to appear in all their splendor. In the past carts were also judged. In 1940 a competition was held at the Teatro Nacional in San Jose with prizes awarded for the best painted carts. This was the last national competition due to the difficulty of bringing the carts to San Jose.

Although there is no longer a national competition, those who appreciate the ox carts always have two other ways in which to judge them: by the music of their wheels and by their colors. It is said that a well painted cart is "bien periqueada", as colorful as a small parakeet. Like the small birds, the bright colors of the ox carts still enliven the roads and landscapes of Costa Rica as they continue to do service as Costa Rica's most famous painted vehicle.

2 - The Buses of Panama

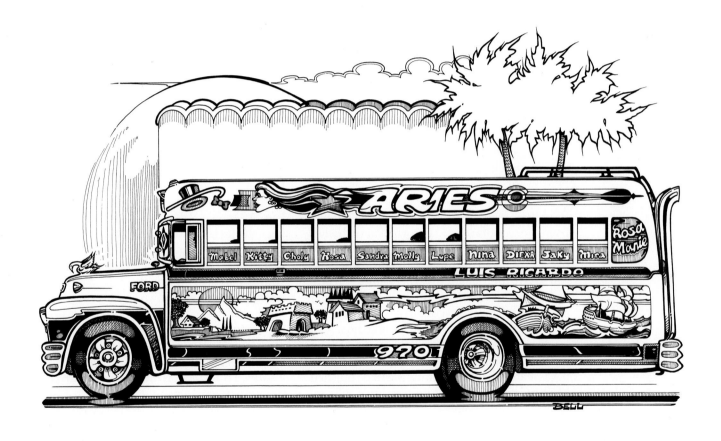

Every school day in the United States thousands of children board sturdy, sober looking buses for their ride between home and class. Yellow is the color for a North American school bus while other colors are used only for the minimal required lettering of bus company name, route, operator and license numbers. But take that same bus south to the Republic of Panama and it soon ceases its color-limited life. Like old-fashioned Neapolitan ice cream a bus will wear a basic three colors (red, white and blue), but otherwise it becomes a Spumoni-creation of special effects. Streamers from the mirrors, flashing lights across the grill work, salsa from the tape deck, elaborate lettering for signs and slogans, and painted decorations everywhere will transform the humble school bus into a Panamanian work of art!

Bus painting began in the 1920's on a smaller vehicle, the chiva, which was a pickup truck with two rows of seats in the back for passengers. The name chiva or chivita refers either to a "goat" from their manner of being driven, or "Chevy" from the manufacturer. The wood or tin bodies of the chivas were first painted with the name of the owner and the route. Later on, owners began to give their small chivas pet names and other decorations to distinguish them and to attract passengers. Chivas served as basic transportation in Panama City until the 1960's, when the school buses arrived to take their place (and to offer a much larger "canvas" for bus art). In the 1970's it was feared that bus painting might be finished when a Government venture introduced still larger buses from Spain. The sleek modernity of these new buses seemed to reject outright any type of painting or slogan and a vibrant form of folk art seemed destined to end. But the Spanish buses proved to be too wide for normal city traffic so the project was not expanded as planned. The gaily painted school buses made

by Ford or Bluebird thus continued to carry passengers throughout Panama City.

Credit for the introduction of bus painting on the chivas and buses is given to an artist known only as "El Lobo", who was practising his skills as early as the 1940's. El Lobo lived in the barrio of Calidonia, but his family had originally come from Barbados or Jamaica, thus providing a possible link with other painted vehicles from the Caribbean area.

Gradually other artists followed El Lobo's lead. Jesus Teodoro de Villarue is regarded by students of bus art as one of the old masters. Villarue, best known by his artistic nom de plume of "Yo Yo", began sketching as a child. He studied graphic design at a school in Panama and took lessons from an art school in Argentina by correspondence. Yo Yo put his training to work doing lettering and numbers for taxis which he also drove, banners for political campaigns, costumes for Carnaval and signs for restaurants, shops and bars. After several decades of experience in painting vehicles large and small (the largest being his most recent work on a helicopter for the Panamanian Army), Yo Yo feels a sense of obligation to younger artists entering the field. Not only has he trained some of his own children in bus painting, but he has completed a series of lessons in the art form. Eighteen buses painted by Yo Yo are labeled "Arte Popular. Leccion XX" on the window of the emergency doors. Each of these lessons, Yo Yo feels, is meant to indicate clearly the proper way to paint a bus.

Along with Yo Yo, two other artists, Ramon Enrique Hormi, or "Monchi", and Andres Salazar, are regarded as among the most important current bus painters. Sandra Eleta, a Panamanian documentary film maker and student of bus art, feels that Monchi does the most conventional work while Salazar, whose style she prefers, has the most Spanish and spiritual concept of subject matter. Monchi's subjects are often taken from the exploits of El Zorro, while Salazar chooses the adventures of Fantomas, the comic strip hero. Each of these three artists receives commissions to paint buses from throughout the city while other lesser known artists may only attract work in their own neighborhoods.

Today, in Panama City, at least ten other artists are active as bus painters. When the Museo de Arte Contemporaneo of Panama City organized a juried competitive exhibition of bus art in 1983, twenty four artists entered their work. "Los Buses de Panama" was the first museum exhibit ever devoted to bus art, but annually at the time of the midwinter Carnaval bus paintings have also been judged and awarded prizes. Three prizes were awarded by the Museo for paintings destined to occupy the space below the window

Buses parked at El Pedregal, one of the terminal points of the bus lines which criss-cross Panama City.

One of "Yo-Yo's" 'Arte Popular" series, photographed on a bus parked at the El Pedregal terminal.

The artist "Yo-Yo", on the porch of his studio, displays a painting for the emergency door of a bus. Included are the Bridge, a dancer in pollera costume, and a painted bus.

Hector Anibal Gomez's painting of the Madonna with Child and infant St. John the Baptist won first prize in the Museo de Arte Contemporaneo competition. Photograph courtesy of the Museum.

The Miraflores locks of the Panama Canal, the Bridge of the Americas, and the Tower in Panama Viejo are combined in Pedro Pablo Ortega's second prize winning emergency door painting. Photograph courtesy of the Museum.

on the rear emergency door. The first prize winner was Hector Anibal Gomez for a religious work entitled "The Madonna of the Chair". Second prize was won by Pedro Pablo Ortega for a patriotic variant of a coat-of-arms called "My Country Panama". "Charles V on Horseback" (after the equestrian portrait by Titian) won third prize for Jose Antonio Enriquez.

The purpose of painting a bus is to attract riders for these privately owned vehicles. Over the years painting has developed from a simple

coat of paint with lettering to the technicolor explosion visible today. Owners are responsible for painting bus numbers and colors indicating the routes. Drivers often suggest additional embellishments, of which landscapes were the earliest. The usual location for these landscapes are the areas above the windows on the front and rear of the bus. Below the landscape on the front windshield the route designation is painted in large, ornamented capital letters. A very typical landscape would show a small wood cottage set among autumn foliage with snow covered peaks in the distance. Yo Yo says that bus owners often prefer exotic, non-Panamanian locales for the landscapes. He, in fact, has painted both the Eiffel Tower and the Statue of Liberty in these small vignettes of the world. For this space bus drivers prefer "algo natural" (something natural), Yo Yo believes. The average Panamanian, Silvano Lora wrote, wants that something natural to show the sea, land and, above all, the Canal. For the city dweller urban ugliness and the difficulties of day-to-day existence are ameliorated by scenes of somewhere else painted on the walls of bars, cantinas and buses. Yo Yo felt that buses which passed through Old Panama or the Canal Zone were more likely to carry painted views of the Tower or the Bridge of the Americas. Owners whose buses travel on routes elsewhere in the city are more apt to choose rural landscapes of memory or those of dream destinations abroad, places they might visit with the money earned from driving the bus.

The side windows of the bus are not always decorated, but when they are they carry the names of girls or, less frequently, the names of the zodiac spray painted or lettered in a single color. What seems to be a fairly new fashion for the windows on the rear of the bus is to spray paint images in silver with the use of stencils.

It is in the larger spaces below the windows on the sides and rear of the bus that an artist's creativity can really shine. Along the two sides

Bus destinations painted on the front windows of a bus are part of the larger composition of landscape, streamers, lights and pinstriping.

The side of a bus becomes the enchanted realm of a mermaid seated below bus windows.

THE BUSES OF PANAMA   33

Looking like the dragons
in Chinese New Year's
parades, this fierce beast
breathes its fury on the
side of a bus.

A sunset gives a warm glow to this fairy tale castle painted on the side panel of a bus.

The door covering the 12 volt battery is decorated with a bird carrying a firecracker.

The thirst or hunger of the bus is emphasized by open mouths and baby bottles which decorate the diesel fuel inlet.

Cartoon characters often find space on bus panels. Wily Carota shown here and Bugs Bunny on the following page are among the examples used by bus painters.

Bus owners may use a portrait of a family member, copied from a photograph, to ornament their buses.

Kaliman, the superhero of Mexican comic books, protects this bus with his extraordinary powers.

of the bus there is easily enough room for another landscape, but the choice here is seldom a cottage in the north woods. Lunar landscapes with strange creatures from other planets, firebreathing dragons, and peculiar beasts from science fiction cavort in the area between the tires. Below them cartoon figures may indicate the location of the battery, or the diesel fuel inlet (the latter often labeled "Comida" or meal).

Above the windows on the bus sides is another long, large space which artists have used for elongated birds, animals and even geometric shapes. Peter Briggs, who tabulated bus paintings in Panama City in 1978, observed that the designs on the upper sides were often hard to see when a bus was moving in traffic. The small landscapes

Rock star Tina Turner smiles from a bus panel painted by "Yo-Yo".

and, above all, anything painted either inside the bus or on the emergency door is far easier to view. Thus, over the years, bus painters have reserved their greatest efforts for the emergency door panels. Entries in the Museo de Arte Contemporaneo competition were all intended for that space.

According to Yo Yo, an artist makes sketches for the emergency door panel from which the bus owner can choose. The subject is most often a single figure composition. It may be a popular singer, television or film star, or a member of the owner's family. Posters, record album covers, and photographs provide images to be enlarged for use on the emergency door panel. Often the name of the subject is included so that bus riders will not forget to ride on the "Tina Turner", "Lucia Mendez" or "Mr. T" bus in the future.

Bus owners who prefer something less secular may opt for portraits of saints or scenes from the life of Christ. A young artist named Fong is known as a specialist in such imagery. Indicative of the importance of the emergency door paintings is the presence of the artist's signature on

A voluptuous lady smiles in another bus panel portrait by "Yo-Yo".

"Mr. T" is here seen in his role from television's "A Team" program.

Characters are often copied from posters advertising movies, as is this portrait of "Rambo", played by Sylvester Stallone.

Even creatures from outer space will find ample space on buses.

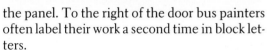

the panel. To the right of the door bus painters often label their work a second time in block letters.

Written decorations are another important form of Panamanian bus art. In 1973 when the larger Spanish buses were introduced, Professor Julio Arosemena and his students in folklore at the University of Panama began what they thought would be a last chance research project on Panamanian bus art. They collected information on both the painted and lettered forms. Their list, organized by bus route and location

Religious subject matter is seen in these paintings of St. Michael the Archangel, and St. Joseph holding the Christ Child. The St. Joseph painting is the work of painter Fong, and is probably modelled on a popular chromolithograph.

Moses holding the Ten Commandments.

"Yo-Yo" varies the wording of his signature, but usually acknowledges the participation of his sons and other assistants.

Lucia Mendez in a sultry pose.

on and within the bus, included 1,783 examples of lettering and 337 paintings. At that time, buses from the San Miguelito and Rio Abajo routes bore the greatest number of lettered phrases and titles. Preferred locations for these inscriptions were inside the bus over a window, on the rear bumper, inside the bus above the front windshield, and around the rear view mirror. Logically, words and phrases on bumpers will be brief because of the space. Slogans or titles decorate bumpers while more lengthy sayings or even poems are painted inside the bus where passengers will have the time to read them. The slogans, sayings, and titles are similar to those found elsewhere in the Americas. Titles of movies and songs are common, but by far the most popular are the sayings ("dichos") which deal with life, love and faith.

"Dichos" include geographical and religious references, advice, and "macho" boasts, but seldom political exhortations. The more personal references found on North American bumper stickers to which they could best be compared (such as support for political viewpoints and candidates, educational affiliations, etc.) are not found in the repertoire of the "rotulo" (lettering) artist.

Another portrait of Lucia Mendez, as "preferred by the public".

sonalized "dichos" would be discouraged or forbidden in favor of corporate uniformity. James Jaquiths wrote that there seemed to be fewer "dichos" of a protective nature than there may have been in the past. He attributes this to a decrease in anxiety among truckers. Improved roads, fewer bandits in isolated areas, and better maintenance of trucks all contributed to this lessening of stress. "Dichos" asking for the protection of God, the Virgin and the various saints were not felt as necessary for bumper decoration by truckers who felt more secure in their work. Many "dichos" recorded by Jaquiths were of a humorous nature, a type also found on Panamanian buses.

According to Nelson Romero, secretary-general of the syndicate of bus owners, there were 2,760 privately owned buses operating in Panama City in 1987. An individual is not supposed to own more than one bus, but that regulation is sometimes evaded by registering buses in the names of other family members. What is painted, lettered or displayed on them is regulated only in terms of the colors which designate the route. Whatever else appears is governed by taste, custom and the owner's pocketbook. Painting a bus may cost between $1,500 and $3,000, depending on the artist and the complexity of the work. The bus may need to be repainted after 3 to 4 years and the work may take up to one week to finish. In addition, there are other costs to be considered for optional decoration: plastic streamers, stainless steel exhaust pipes, additional colored and blinking lights, and music. After an initial investment of $30,000 or more for the bus itself, the owner may easily spend upwards of $5,000 more for decorating before he is ready to place his bus into service.

When the newly painted bus rolls off down the Via España or the Avenida Central of Pana-

Those who have studied similar "dichos" found on Mexican truck bumpers have noted changes in the names and expressions used over the years. Gloria Giffords pointed out that, as more trucks are owned by companies rather than individuals, the custom of painting and personalizing trucks through "dichos" would probably die out. Companies choose standardized colors and use their own logos. The use of per-

Singer Janet Jackson rides above a personal bumper slogan. Graphic designs on the edges of the bumpers often resemble the markings of pinball or slot machines seen in Panamanian casinos.

ma City with streamers flying from the rear view mirror, salsa music playing, and paintings glistening in the sun, it will be as up-to-date an expression of popular taste as its owners could hope for. In words and images, as Sandra Eleta says, it will offer to the world a mirror of the artist's soul, the soul of Panama.

3 - The Tap-Taps of Haiti

"Tap-Tap" means hurry in the Creole language of Haiti and hurry is just what converted trucks do as they seek passengers in the streets of Port-au-Prince. Expanded, painted and decorated the "Tap-Taps", as these trucks are known, provide public transportation in the capital and to Haiti's other cities. The decorating of Tap-Taps began in the late 1940's, probably stimulated by the painting of a jeep belonging to the Centre d'Art Gallery in Port-au-Prince. The custom of naming vehicles and of painting houses, signs and

A shop on the Petionville road hangs papier mache Tap-Taps on the wall to attract tourist buyers. Photograph by Cathy Holmberg.

murals had, however, long been a part of Haiti's artistic heritage.

Like the ox cart in Costa Rica, the Tap-Tap is mentioned in virtually every book written about Haiti. Visitors marvel at their colors and names. Haiti's artists have painted them and portrayed them in paintings and watercolors. Craftsmen make small Tap-Taps in wood, metal and papier-mache. But, with the exception of a single research paper written by Gerald Alexis and others in 1981, little effort has been made to document or understand the Tap-Taps. Much of the historical background in this chapter is derived from this study by M. Alexis, now the Directeur of the Musee du Pantheon National, and his colleagues, and from a series of local histories written by Georges Corvington.

Although the first privately owned automobile reached Port-au-Prince in the year 1909, public transportation by motorized vehicle developed only as quickly as adequate roads made this possible. For most Haitians living in Port-au-Prince, a tramway with three kilometers of track and horse drawn buggies (known as the "buss") were the major means of transportation until the 1920's. In the countryside people walked.

During the American military occupation of Haiti (1915-1934) some roads were built, but as James Leyburn wrote in 1940, driving on them was a very bumpy experience. Since Port-au-Prince, Cap Haitien, and Jacmel, the major towns of Haiti, were seaports, Leyburn helpfully suggested that visitors would be much more comfortable if they did their sightseeing by boat rather than by car. By the 1920's an entrepreneur named Cameau was using Ford and Chevrolet trucks to transport both people and goods. The trucks were fitted with two or three wooden benches for passengers, given a one color paint job, and labelled with the company name. These trucks drove within Port-au-Prince and as far south as Leogane. Passengers could buy either first or second class tickets depending on how much baggage they were carrying.

By the year 1930 other companies (Marcel Tourreau and Pepe Delva) were driving modified trucks with passenger seats. Delva's "char-a-bancs" took the hilly road to Petionville, 1500 feet above Port-au-Prince. Edna Taft, an American writer who rode a char-a-banc from Port-au-Prince to Croix-des-Bouquets in 1938, noted the hardness of the seats, the jolting of the vehicle and bus names such as "Dieu avec nous", "Immaculee", "Saint Joseph" and "Toussaint Louverture". Such names are still being used today.

With the coming of World War II, imports into Haiti of trucks, cars and replacement parts ceased. The Cameau firm kept its trucks running by "cannibalizing" parts, using salvagable parts from old trucks to create new ones. At this time wooden truck bodies were usually built by men experienced as boat builders.

After the war the stratagem of necessity became one of preference as other entrepreneurs modified small pick-up trucks with wooden enclosures. These wooden additions, known locally as "habitats", needed to be painted for durability and, gradually, the development of the painted designs led to the full kaleidoscopic panoply of Tap-Tap art in the 1980's.

Public transport currently found in Haiti relies on two sizes of Tap-Taps, and upon long distance trucks which can carry cargo as well as passengers, all heaped on the top. All of these vehicles are painted, decorated and named.

The smallest size of Tap-Tap was originally based on the American pick-up truck body. Today that body is more likely to be of Japanese manufacture, with Nissan, Daihatsu, Mazda, Mitsubishi, Toyota, and Isuzu among the companies noted. There is one seat within the cab and an open cargo back when the vehicle is originally delivered. Transformation of the vehicle begins with the removal of the tailgate by cutting it in half, and then reassembling both parts with the former outer edges now forming the inner sides. A space is left in the middle through which the passengers will enter, and seats will also be built above the re-arranged tailgate sections. Benches are then placed along the sides of the cargo area. Finally, an entire superstructure of wood is built over and above the cargo area. Usually this wooden "habitat" is left open in places for ventilation.

"Voici Baby", a bois fouille or larger size Tap-Tap as seen in Port-au-Prince.

Some Tap-Taps carry canvas which can be rolled down in case of rain. The wooden habitat is composed of horizontal slats which are carved with geometric shapes. These shapes are painted blue, yellow, green and red on a white background, with paint being so thickly applied that the relief is often difficult to make out.

Below, on both sides of the metal body, painters often place three images. These may vary from truck to truck but they often include a pair of flamingos or a swan behind the rear tires, doves in the middle, and a lion on the front door. The swans and doves are also used by sign painters to decorate the small "borlette" booths where bets are placed in most Haitian markets.

Tap-Taps have names painted in the space above the front windows and above the rear entrance. Front and back names are seldom identical. The name of the Tap-Tap builder and the route it travels are usually painted along the sides. Some Tap-Taps carry a small wooden sign protruding jauntily from their roofs, to indicate whether they are heading for the airport, Delmas, or Carrefour.

Tap-Taps may have added hood ornaments, decorative grillwork, bumper decorations and lights. At Christmas, according to Gerald Alexis, Tap-Tap drivers string tree lights over the roofs of their small trucks, so that the streets glow with rolling "arbres de Noel."

The next larger size of Tap-Tap is the "bois fouille" or simply "bus" which is also built on a truck body. This time the entire metal rear body of the truck is removed and replaced with a complete superstructure of wood. The wood is either pine or oak, mostly imported from the Dominican Republic. Entrance to this vehicle is from the side. Normal capacity for this size Tap-Tap is 32 passengers. The greater size of this vehicle offers many more possibilities for decoration. These

A serene swan painted just behind the rear tire of a small Tap-Tap.

A pair of swans from the body of another small Tap-Tap.

Doves like this one are painted on borlette betting booths.

Lions are often painted on the doors of Tap-Taps like this beast with his grillwork mane.

Wheels, hood
ornaments and
bumper
metalwork are
all painted on
this Tap-Tap.

The building of a Tap-Tap begins with a wooden superstructure.

"Relax and enjoy the ride", seems to be the message of this Tap-Tap door painting.

Tap-Taps have glass windows as well as carved and painted wooden slat sides; the sides often have additional turned carpentry details such as spindles or scallops. Below the rear window is a large space on which appears a more important painting. This painting, like the emergency door paintings on the Panamanian buses, is easily visible and can be produced by the most skilled artist. Here can be found religious scenes, events, portraits, and stars from movies, music and television.

Like the smaller Tap-Tap, the bus carries its name in the same location back and front. Its route is usually indicated along one side, sometimes within an electrified light panel. The name of the builder may be prominently written on the rear of the bus, while the painter/ designer and even the electrician will also sign their names on the sides.

Tap-Taps are built in integrated workshops in Port-au-Prince. That is, virtually all of the reconstruction and painting is handled by the same firm. The customer need only supply the truck body and specify the kind of decoration preferred. Each stage in the creation of the Tap-Tap will be the province of one craftsman: metal worker, carpenter, upholsterer, electrician, artist/ designer and assistant artist. In most workshops Tap-Taps in all stages of construction and repair are crowded so closely together that workers can barely squeeze between them. At the same time a metal worker is cutting the tailgate apart, a carpenter may be carving the geometric frieze, and painters will be working on nearly finished Tap-Taps. Assistant painters work in one color at a time, filling in the red, blue, yellow or green details. The artist/ designer does the large painting on the rear of the vehicle. Richard Coeur Sensible, Oreste and Wilfrid Nicholas are among the more skilled Tap-Tap painters. In all, seven of

Tap-Tap decoration can include a scalloped entrance door, carved floral decorations, spindles and wrapped hand grips.

A pastoral scene appealed to Lyla's owner.

Yvon Tibabing built this Tap-Tap named "Magnum" after the popular detective program hero. The beach scene probably refers to the Hawaiian setting of this television program.

Two sides of a large Tap-Tap suggest the complex nature of the design. The destination of this Tap-Tap is Carrefour Road.

The owner of a Tap-Tap
built by Frenel Methelus
chose a religious theme. Fan
Fan did the electrical work.

Wilfrid Nicholas is a
painter in Okel Ultimo's
workshop.

such workshops were inspected during our visit to Port-au-Prince. Others exist, of course, but minor repairs and repainting may also done quite casually in the street, or wherever needed.

According to the Alexis study, the first scenes painted on Tap-Taps were the work of Alex Roy (or Wah) who completed these pioneering efforts between 1948 and 1952. The Centre d'Art jeep was painted for the first time in 1947. According to Seldon Rodman, an early director of the Centre, the jeep was white-washed and painted over by the artists three times during that first year. Now, according to Francine Murat, Directrice of the Centre since 1967, the jeep exists only in photographs. The jeep-painting was a collaborative effort by painters then working at the Centre. This jeep provided an important inspiration for the Tap-Tap painters who had previously limited themselves to doing names and small floral decorations.

St. Joseph holding the
Christ Child is based on a
popular print.

subject matter is more reliant on current fashion. Thus, Rambo appears on a Tap-Tap as does the winged horse logo of the Tri Star Film Company. These paintings might well be replaced with more up-to-the-moment film references as time passes.

While artists who sell their work through Haiti's many art galleries may once have painted Tap-Taps, today most of them do not. An article by Clyde Farnsworth in The New York Times noted, however, that necessity might well make Tap-Tap painting a welcome option once again. After cruise ships stopped calling at Cap Haitien, for example, at least some of that city's painters

The patron saint of
travelers, St. Christopher,
is an appropriate choice
for a Tap-Tap painting.

The choice of subject matter for Tap-Tap art is made by the customer who decides what he would like his vehicle to show. He may even provide religious chromolithographs or other printed images to be copied. Some of the same saintly lithographs are used as sources for both Tap-Tap and Panamanian bus imagery. These lithographs, printed in Mexico, are widely available for sale in the streets and markets of Haiti. Religious images are probably chosen over and over in each repainting of the Tap-Tap. Other

The popularity of "Rambo", Sylvester Stallone's violent hero, is noted in Haiti as well as in Panama.

The winged horse logo of a movie company conveys a sense of speed and an interest in films.

The baptism of Christ was painted in Mario Arnault's Tap-Tap yard.

returned to Tap-Tap painting. The expansion of Tap-Tap routes there has also brought an increase in such jobs.

The cost of painting a Tap-Tap in 1987 ranges from $300 to $400 for the smallest size to $600 to $800 for the larger "bois 'fouille". The wooden superstructure would cost $2,500 or more, while any wiring or sound equipment would result in still extra costs. Mario Arnault, whose workshop is located along the Rue Magasin de l'Etat, said he completes between 150 and 175 Tap-Taps each year. His firm, begun by his father, has been in business for thirty five years. Probably the largest firm in Port-au-Prince is that of Okel Ultimo on the Boulevard de Dessalines. Called the General Motors of the Tap-Tap industry by Gerald Alexis, Ultimo converted buses have an easily recognized pattern of geometric bands below the side windows. One wider band typically includes a pair of faces, birds and flowers.

A tabulation of words and names recorded

Typical design
for the side of
an Okel
Ultimo
Tap-Tap.

Jean Paul Belmondo, the French film star, is featured on the rear of this Tap-Tap. His name was on the front.

er of Youth). Names were of the owner ("Hubert No. 1"), a friend or family member ("Anne Cherie" or "This is Tania"), or a famous individual ("Belmondo", "Al Capone", or "Maradona" the soccer player). Occasionally a phrase such as "Merci Maman" (Thanks, Mom) might be used to suggest the assistance of someone else in making the Tap-Tap enterprise possible. Family involvement was also indicated by Tap-Tap names such as "Trois Freres" (Three Brothers) or, on a large truck, "La Famille Capoise" for an enterprise based in Cap Haitien.

The religious content of Tap-Tap names clearly indicates to passengers whether the owner is a Roman Catholic, Protestant, or Voodoo follower. Passengers can then choose or reject a ride on the basis of belief. Names of saints ("St. Antoine", "Ste. Rose of Lima", "St. Joseph", "St. Louis", and "St. Pierre"), references to specific Biblical verses ("Romains 15: 7", "Exode 14: 14" and "Psaumes 1"), places ("Jerusalem Cite Celeste") and pious counsel all could be listed under the banner of faith.

Among the statements of faith were those such as "Priez Dieu" (Pray to God), "Dieu est Bon" (God is Good), "Christ Revient Bientot" (Christ is returning soon), and "Aime ton prochain comme toi meme" (Love your neighbor as yourself). Clearly the choice of wording such as "Dieu me protege" (May God protect me), "Dieu guide mes pas" (May God guide my steps), and "A Pran'n La Vie" (Learn from life), and frequent selection of Christ as the Good Shepherd for the large door paintings suggest the same wish for protection of the Tap-Tap and its passengers. This wish was once common, for example, among the slogans painted on Mexican truck bumpers, as noted by James R. Jaquith. The hazards of driving and the condition of the Haitian roads certainly warrant this concern.

on Tap-Taps which passed on the Boulevard Dessalines, the Avenue Delmas, Avenue John Brown (the road to Petionville), and the highway to Cap Haitien, suggests the following conclusions. Words and names written in Spanish, English or Creole were noted, but the overwhelming majority were in French. If these words and names were then classified by type, those of a religious nature would be the most popular, followed by indicators of places, proper names, and concepts such as "Perseverance" or "Fleur de Jeunesse" (Flow-

"With Jesus" is a typical example of religious wording in Tap-Tap names.

"Christ as the good Shepherd" is a scene of tranquility often chosen for Tap-Tap doors and side panels.

Religious names on Tap-Taps often have more than one possible interpretation. Gemini is a sign of the zodiac but may also refer to the Twins (Marassa) of Voodoo belief, as do the French words "Les Jumeaux" (The Twins). Similarly, a portrait of the Virgin and Child is seen as that of Erzulie Dantor, the Voodoo goddess of love. Voodoo, in Haiti, is a syncretic religion blending beliefs and deities from Africa (Dahomey, Nigeria, and Zaire) with those of Roman Catholicism in new interpretations. Thus, names and images may be understood in different ways, depending upon the belief of the beholder.

Several Tap-Taps bearing the place names of "Mt. Carmel" and of "Altagracia" refer to important pilgrimage sites for Catholics in Haiti. The Virgin of Miracles, also called Our Lady of Mont Carmel, reputedly appeared several times in palm trees at Saut d'Eau near the village of Ville Bonheur during the 19th century and once again during the American military occupation. Pilgrimages to Saut d'Eau take place on July 16th. The waterfall at Saut d'Eau which tumbles among mossy trees and ferns has also long been known as the home of Damballah-wedo, the Voodoo serpent god who dwells near springs and marshes. Followers of Damballah, of his wife Ayida and of other aquatic deities also make the trip to Saut d'Eau. In a different Latin American country James Kus noted the use of the "Cruz de Chalpon" on Peruvian bus bumpers and discovered that it was the name of an important Peruvian festival whose date and site had been celebrated since PreColumbian times when it was the feast of Pachamama.

Political names or slogans were not found among Tap-Tap names which, given Haiti's current uncertain political climate, is understandable. One Tap-Tap did bear the words "Avec union nap viv" (In union there is strength), taken from Haiti's coat-of-arms. There were also few of the bragging or sexually linked names that researchers have found on truck bumpers elsewhere in Latin America, although "The Loving Bus", "Kiss Me Baby" and "Sweet Woman" were noted. Hugh Cave wrote that Ti Cousin, the late houngan (Voodoo priest) of Leogane once owned Tap-Taps, one of which he named "Neg'sot" (Silly Negroes), but such names were probably the exception even in Ti Cousin's day. Business is too precarious an endeavor to risk alienating the customer by one's choice of a Tap-Tap name.

One of the reasons which Gerald Alexis gave for having prepared his report on Tap-Taps was the concern over the future of the vehicles. As in Panama, a new vehicle has made its entrance on the market. This vehicle is the Japanese mini-van, which can carry passengers in far greater comfort and needs no transformation. In fact, it even seems to reject paint, so that owners are content to decorate their new vans only with decals. So far these vans co-exist with the traditional Tap-Taps, although the vans do now seem to be in the majority on the Petionville route. Sadly for lovers of Tap-Tap art, the only painted decoration on these vans is the names.

Names, slogans, flowers, birds and lions are all a part of the art of the Tap-Tap. One anony-

mous Tap-Tap artist included his own opinion on the vehicle. Carefully written in script above the rear tire of a small size Tap-Tap were the words "La critique est aisee mais l'art est difficile" (Criticism is easy but art is difficult), a statement shared by artists the world over.

A vigilant eagle perched on a rifle is outlined in the same style as the walking lion, noted in an earlier illustration.

4 - The Kustom Cars of The United States

Every spring and summer weekend lead sleds cruise in stately procession to meets and rallyes held in parking lots or fair grounds across the United States. "Slow and low" are part of the aesthetic followed in transforming American-made sedans, convertibles, coupes, roadsters and even pickup trucks. These cars, built between 1935 and 1964, are rebuilt, repainted and modified according to a very individual and specific canon of taste. What was originally produced by General Motors, Ford or Chrysler is now a mixture of grilles, bumpers, engines, headlights and taillights from various other makes, models and years. Although custom cars with special features could always be purchased from the manufacturer, the "kustom" car is something else entirely. The lead sled is one form of a "kustom" or customized car; hot rods and street machines are the other examples of stock model cars rebuilt by their owners. The results are often unique and creative examples of personal taste. As one observer put it, "It is art, not transportation".

Within the "Kustom" car world there are two roads to follow: not high or low, but fast or slow. Those who transform cars into hot rods or street machines aim for speed. Those who build lead sleds (and their Hispanic counterpart, the low rider) are more concerned with aesthetics, comfort and a lowered but leisurely ride. As the personalized license plate of a 1950 Mercury put it, "Drop Um", and that's just what lead sled owners do to their cars, changing the suspension so the car barely clears the pavement.

In the history of cars the hot rods (or street rods, as they are now usually called) came first. The cheapest and most plentiful cars to transform into rods were the Fords of the early 1930's. Off came bumpers, fenders and running boards. In went a new engine, often a Ford V8 flathead, which could supply the desired speed. Hoods were omitted so that the new engine could be seen in all of its polished glory. Better tires, small in front and large in back, helped the new rod burn rubber on the road. The final finishing touch was to paint the rod, sometimes in a solid color, but often with flames which spread their spirals from the engine back along the doors of the car for an added sense of speed. Black was considered the traditional body color with flames beginning in yellow, shading to orange, and ending in red at the point of each fiery lick of flame.

The hot rod phenomenon began in the 1930's in California where good weather, places to race, and a large number of cars to improve were all available. Cynthia Golub Dettelbach suggested in her book, "In the Driver's Seat" that the Fords and later, Chevrolets, which became hot rods were driven to California by families fleeing Dust Bowl conditions for jobs and a better life further west. These cars found new owners and new lives in California as well.

Automobile racing has long been popular as a very expensive sport in the United States and in Europe. What the hot rodder did was to create his own vehicle and find his own track: a city street, a dry lake bed, or an unused airport land-ing strip. Racing in town or in the country became so popular with the rodders during the 1930's that clubs were organized to sponsor, promote and regulate these activities. The Southern California Timing Association (1937) was the first such group. Later, clubs were formed for those interested in street rods, street machines and lead sleds. Races, rallyes, swap meets and "how-to-do-it" information filled the pages of periodicals published for those who repaired, rebuilt and collected such cars. "Hot Rod", "Rod and Custom", "Road and Track" and "Street Rodder" magazines shared the newsstand with many other titles aimed at readers who wanted to know more about specific models or types of cars. Most recently, car shows have been recorded on video cassettes.

The division between street rod, street machine and lead sled is sometimes difficult to make. Both rods and machines are cars transformed for speed. Rods are often cars from the early 1930's (usually Fords), while machines can be late models of any make, although the 1955-1957 Chevrolets are often selected. Mercurys from the 1950 to 1955 era are favorite choices for lead sleds. With all three types the goal is to create a new vehicle, not to restore the car to its original condition.

When Jerry Titus founded the national KKOA (Kustom Kemps of America) organization in 1980, he used this alternate term for the lead sled. "Kustom Kemp" was supposed to have been used first by a cartoon character in the May, 1959 issue of "Rod and Custom" magazine. Actor Ed

"Kookie" Byrnes, the parking lot attendant in television's "77 Sunset Strip" also popularized the name. In the most recent "Lead Sled Spectacular" of the KKOA, held in Springfield, Illinois during July of 1987, only sleds from 1935 to 1964 could be entered in competition.

For some people lead sleds are inextricably linked to the 1950's. This idea is promoted by those who organize "Back to the '50's" car shows where Elvis Presley and Chuck Berry records are played over the public address system and in the evening participants cruise to local drive-ins or attend "sock-hop" dances. "Cruising" once meant simply driving around with no particular destination or purpose in mind. Cruising was a happening in which any teenager with a car could join. Today, at weekend car shows, the "cruise" is an evening parade for all of the registered cars. Car owners also stress the fifties theme in the names which they choose for their sleds, names

"Forties Forever" it says on the dashboard of Gene Sonnen's 1940 Ford coupe. In the area behind the steering wheel Dave Bell painted the car itself (named "Red" after Mrs. Sonnen) with its classic flame job.

troubles even forty years ago), a "carro bajo" seemed to defy any danger in its slow retreat, ignoring the violence in the same way that a matador turns his back in the bull ring and walks away from the bull. Low riders (and low rider clubs) are found in cities throughout the Southwest. "Q-vo" magazine deals with the "carros" and the "vatos" and "pachucos" who drive them. Cars which become low riders are painted with fade-away, muted colors and occasionally with murals which sometimes include religious scenes. These cars usually retain their chrome and have crushed vel-

Under the lavender striped hood of Paul Knapp's 1953 Oldsmobile is this small painting of a carhop, roller skating on the job at Tubby's Drive-in. The "Menu" lists the specifications of the Knapp car which is seen pulling up at her left. The painting was done by M. K. John of Muscatine, Iowa.

like "Yakkity Yak", "Blue Moon", "Misty Blue", and "The Big Bopper".

A low rider is another purposely slow moving car. According to Peggy Beck, the low rider tradition began in Los Angeles among Mexican immigrants in the 1930's. Lowering their "carros bajos" allowed them to cruise slowly in a motorized form of the traditional "paseo", which took place around and in the village squares of old Mexico. There was perhaps another more fatalistic quality to slowing the low rider. In case of an altercation (and there were plenty of street gang

The spare tire cover (or, "Continental kit") is a perfect place either for a car's name or for a nostalgic scene.

vet and tooled leather interiors. Chevrolets were among the earliest low riders, while Buick Rivieras seem favored today.

In modifying their cars, customizers often "chop" (lower the roof and door pillars), "channel" (lower the car body on its frame by cutting the floor loose and then re-welding it into a different position), and "section" (remove a horizontal section around the entire body of the car). They "de-chrome" by removing all chrome trim and badges. The resulting holes in the body are filled with plastic or lead (hence the term "lead sled").

Named for a song, "Yakkity Yak", this 1960 Chrysler was painted white with thin red scallops by its owner, Larry Grobe of Lombard, Illinois. The images on the spare tire cover explain the name.

Stock bumpers may be replaced by other bumpers considered more pleasing in the overall design. Headlights, taillights and aerials may be replaced, hooded, or "frenched" (recessed into the car body). Even hubcaps are changed in the process of making over the car. One lead sled owner proudly claimed that parts from 22 other cars were now built into his vehicle. For rods and machines the goal is a streamlined, fast appearance. For the lead sled, extraneous details are removed to create a smooth, uninterrupted line on these somewhat pudgy, bulky vehicles.

Lowering a car is in tune with American taste. Phil Patton wrote in "Open Road" that Americans had "an almost mystic reverence for the horizontal . . . the line of the prairie, of the beckoning horizon . . . the line of destiny manifested." Highways, Prairie School houses, and car design all strive for such an earth bound, wind resistant line. Early cars, based on coaches and carriages, were built high off the ground with a tall silhouette and enough interior height so that passengers could ride wearing their tallest hats, without bumping against the roof. In the 1930's Harley Earl's designs for General Motors cars as well as the Chrysler Airflow car reduced that overall height, creating a design which was lower and more streamlined. The lead sled and the hot rod, with variant goals, thus follow a basic American aesthetic preference.

California customizers like George and Sam Barris, Neil Emery, Gene Winfield, and Ed "Big Daddy" Roth originated many of these bodywork techniques. Cars such as Barris' "Golden Sahara" (a 1954 Lincoln coupe with a plexiglass roof) and Emery's "Polynesian" (a 1950 Oldsmobile) were famous throughout the country from their appearances at car shows and the descriptions of them in car magazines. Tom Wolfe, in his essay on the customizing scene, "The Kandy*Kolored

"Fine 39" is the license plate for Connie Winkler's 1939 brown Mercury coupe. Its free form scallops emphasize the chopped and lowered silhouette.

Tangerine*Flake Streamline Baby", refers to their work as not that of building cars, but of creating forms, like sculpture. Barris and Roth also designed models to be reproduced in kits by model makers (AMT and Revell) so that new generations of car enthusiasts could try to build miniatures before graduating to full size projects.

For the mild or wild "Kustom" car, painting is the final touch and that, too, developed originally in California. Von Dutch, Tommy the Greek, Dean Jeffries, Larry Watson and Joe Bailon were among the pioneers noted for their abilities as pinstripers and flame painters on vehicles of all kinds. One of the best known flame jobs

decorates Pete Chapouris' "California Kid", a 1934 Ford painted in the traditional color combination.

Customizers who had rebuilt cars in ways unimagined (but often later imitated) by Detroit would obviously not be content with the paint colors Detroit had used for its nitrocellulose lacquer and super enamel paints. There was not enough variety and sometimes these paints faded or cracked. The glistening shades of paint used on drums inspired Joe Bailon and George Barris to develop the first "candy apple" paints, called that for their resemblance to caramel coated candied apples. Candy apple acrylic lacquers are

Along the sides of this 1957 Chevrolet lowrider pickup are wide bands of color. On the tailgate a few "carros bajos" cruise past downtown Phoenix under a starry blue sky. The car was painted in Phoenix, Arizona, but photographed in Minnesota.

Deep greens are appropriate colors for the scallops on this 1949 Oldsmobile named "Toad" by its owner, Doug Reed of Wichita, Kansas.

spray painted over a primer and a base. The base paint used can be white pearl, black pearl or one of the metallic shades such as gold, silver or bronze. Combinations of various candy colors with the bases give a translucent glow which shines through the numerous coats of clear acrylic lacquer which covers them.

Other options for the custom painter are flake paints (with mylar particles suspended in either clear or candy lacquers) or pearl paints. Pearls are made either from ground herring scales or lead salt crystals. Pearls come in concentrate or paste forms to be mixed with clear acrylic lacquer or, like the flakes, with the candy colors before being sprayed over the base paints.

Spray painting the candy colors, flakes and pearls involves careful sanding of the surface between coats of the lacquers and close attention to the handling of the equipment to avoid bubbles, blistering and fisheye cracking. Many paint companies include custom paints for cars among their lines. A few companies, such as House of Kolor, Ditzler and Metalflake, specialize in automotive paints. Paint manufacturer Jon Kosmoski of Minneapolis developed many new paint colors and then produced books and video cassettes to explain the proper techniques for using them. As he says, "preparation is important because you can't build a good house on a swamp". The swatches for the paints which Kosmoski sells through his House of Kolor show how each candy color changes, depending on the nature of its underlying base.

The candy colors and clear lacquers can be sprayed to completely cover the car in even coats or the painter can place masking tape and stencils to create other effects. Areas of color which fade into each other can be planned with tape, as can flames and scallops.

Pinstriping, another traditional form of car

Candy apple paints were the first coats on this 1975 Ford Ranchero pickup. Dale Laroche of Blaine, Minnesota, painted the "Comanchero". Flames seem to grow out of the Indian warrior's carefully painted hair and headband.

During the Lead Sled Spectacular painter M. K. John added pinstriped scrolls and flourishes to the headlights and trunk of one participant's car. John, a self-taught artist, designed the official T shirts for this Springfield, Illinois show.

painting, is done by hand, using a tapered brush often called a "dagger brush". The pinstripe line (like the thin white line woven into mens' dark suit fabric) can serve as a border between flames and the background colors on a vehicle, but it can also lead a life of its own. Pinstripes become calligraphic explosions of line in the hands of an expert. Von Dutch was noted for the way in which faces, eyes and leaves grew out of his pinstripes. Some of the most complex pinstriping highlights the area on the trunk where the car's emblem once rested. Similar bursts of entwined lines find

Pinstriping can outline windows and bumpers, draw attention to taillights and frenched aerials, and become a focal point in this elaborate trunk design photographed at the Lead Sled Spectacular.

their way onto hoods and to the former locations of door handles. The "frenched" recess for an aerial often calls for a spider's web spreading out from the hole. Pinstripers often choose "one step", an enamel paint used by sign painters.

Airbrushed murals are another form of car painted decoration. Hoods and trunks were the location for most murals on cars during the 1970's. Today, murals are most often painted on vans which boast etched and stenciled glasswork as well.

Many car owners name their vehicles, carrying out the chosen theme in upholstery and other decoration. The "Black Widow" (a 1951 Ford) had spider's webs in red on its black body. A 1950 Mercury was painted a deep cornflower blue, evoking its song-title name, "Blue Moon". Seats are covered with tuck and roll naugahyde in appropriate colors, the dashboards can sport tooled leather or a bit of pinstriping, and fuzzy plush dice hang from the rear view mirror. Dice, implying a racer's feeling of gambling with death, have been featured on car mirrors from the early days. Now, they come in many sizes and colors, but once, said a spectator at the Lead Sled Spectacular, "the only kind of dice you could possibly have were black and white."

Pinstripes, flames, murals and small cartoon figures are all included in car art of the 1980's. Today, says artist Dave Bell, "there is a real Renaissance of car painting". A carefully done paint job is expensive, but can last for years. In the northern states, painted lead sleds and street rods often spend the months between November and April inside the garage. In milder climates these cars venture forth year round. Rick Chronic of Oklahoma City takes pride in driving his flame painted 1956 Ford Victoria to work every day. Weather doesn't pose as great a problem in Okla-

homa, but drivers who keep their eyes on his car rather than on the road do, he says.

Car painting is often a lengthy process. The flames on Rick Chronic's car were taped and painted during an all-night painting session so that the car would be ready to drive in a parade the following morning. A three-color graphic pattern for the sides and hood of a 1958 Pontiac Starchief took seventy-two hours to complete, said Don Treble who did the work. It wasn't the actual painting which took so long, but the careful taping of the layout of color bands. The Daytona-style racing checks of "Wave Rider" (a 1970 Volkswagen) took Patrick Lehman a month to tape and paint. Multi-colored patterns take time to tape, time to spray, and time to dry. Thus, artists who use the spray gun for scallops and flames, or the airbrush (its smaller relative) for murals, need more time for their work than do pinstripers

Realistic landscapes are popular choices for murals on vans.

Yellow flames thread their way between bands of louvers on the hood of Rick Chronic's 1956 Ford Victoria. Pinstriping outlines the bursts of flames along the sides of the car, which was painted by Rick Knight of Oklahoma City.

This 1940 Ford was entry number one in the first Street Rods National meet. The intricate pinstripes were painted by Dave Bell in 1967. With care, they look almost new twenty years later.

who can design the layout with a pencil and bring the line to life with a dagger brush full of paint.

Custom painters charge between $25 and $35 per hour for their work, comparable, said one very old guide to custom painting, to the fees once received by a doctor or a lawyer. Custom painting began in California, but today it is a national art form. Some car owners do their own painting while others commission work from professionals, occasionally trading a paint job for upholstery, carpentry, or body work. Custom paint jobs have lasted as long as a decade, but most painters would expect their work to last only as long as the car's original coat of paint. Custom

painting is a specialized skill, yet most of these artists are self-taught. Like Water Rat, who messed around with boats in "The Wind in the Willows", car painters often messed around with cars as teenagers, learning as they went along how to rebuild an engine or install a new grille. Painting could be learned, as well, and those with talent found themselves with a hobby-turned profession. Often their own cars served as the first announcement of their ability as painters. Participating in car shows was another way for many of the painters to publicise their work. Most of those who paint cars and trucks (and vans, motorbikes, boats, snowmobiles, airplanes and

The bands of color on George Harris' 1958 Pontiac Starchief make this lead sled appear even lower than hydraulics can make it. The car was photographed at the "50's Nationals", a car show held in Anoka, Minnesota.

Some flame patterns involve overlays. These red flames on Sonny Venuti's 1950 Mercury are carefully separated and outlined with pinstriping by Karl Kelsey of Beverly, Massachusetts.

now, even helicopters) don't really need to adver-
tize; there is plenty of referral work from satisfied
customers or body shops. An Iowa based custom
painter, M. K. John, is sure that the pinstripes he
has painted so far could stretch from Seattle to
Poughkeepsie. Most artists sign their work. Jerry Thomson of St. Paul, uses his CB handle,
"Creeper" as identification, and symbolizes his
name with a small bare foot painted at the edge
of his images.

There are other spinoffs for car painters as
well. Some, like Dave Bell, do cartoons for national magazines. His "Henry Hirise" cartoon for
"Street Rodder" magazine has even inspired fans
to build cars modelled on those which he had
drawn. For each car show there is an artist-
designed button, poster, T-shirt and bill cap.
Plain, white T-shirts and clean tight jeans were
the teenage uniform of the fifties. With the
popularity of commemorative T-shirts, screen
printed or airbrushed for every possible event or
place, car enthusiasts who once wore plain white
shirts now promote their hobby in vivid color. But
when motorbikers gather each year at Daytona,
Florida or Sturgis, South Dakota, their T-shirts
are black with screen printed designs and slogans.

What is painted on cars has changed over
the years. Pinstriping was the first technique.
Thin lines of contrasting colors were used to outline and accent car sections on factory models
from the 1920's on. Flames burst forth, so to
speak, on drag racers in the 1930's. They were a
familiar motif on hot rods and lead sleds by the
1950's, with licks in many colors besides the earliest red-orange-yellow combination. Panels filled
with continuous lines or patterns made with various stencils were popular in the 1960's. By the
1970's murals had found their way onto van
panels, truck tailgates and muscle car hoods. Airbrushed murals are often inspired by science

"Come and try it!", the
warning on Paul
Bloomquist's Toyota
truck, is flanked by two
belligerent bulldogs. Jerry
Thomson (aka "Creeper")
painted the words and
beasts on the tailgate.

Creeper painted a long
bearded character
wearing a ten gallon hat
above each rear tire of
Greg Kriegelmeyer's
Cherokee Chief truck.

M. K. John painted these science fiction characters, a dragon-riding equestrienne and three cave men, upon the tailgate of a 1981 Chevrolet pickup. Photographs courtesy of M. K. John.

fiction with movie posters and record albums providing adaptable images. In the 1980's all of the earlier styles and techniques are still in use. Some car owners are happy with just a bit of pinstriping and a cartoon character or two to suggest the name or personality of the car.

Perhaps the largest number of cars which were custom painted for a single owner were those belonging to a cult leader in Oregon. The Bhagwan Shree Rajneesh, whose followers lived in the town of Antelope, owned eighty five Rolls Royces. One of his disciples, a former car painter from Southern California who took the reli-

gious name of Swami Deva Peter, painted all of the Bhagwan's fleet. The designs were Asian in feeling (cranes, peacocks, and kimonos) and were conceived as if the cars had been flattened and viewed from above. Each air brushed design was painted across the entire car. After the Bhagwan's enterprise was closed, the cars were sold to a Texas firm.

As is the case with the other painted vehicles in this book, the custom car world is basically masculine. Although women are astronauts, pilots and race car drivers they are not often seen working as bodyshop mechanics, garage owners or even as car painters. However, women do participate in the clubs and shows, and put their skills to work on car interiors. As a woman at the Springfield show commented, "We love to cruise around in our car. It's really a family affair." For her, a husband's interest had become a shared source of family pride.

Growing up in America during the age of the automobile has come to involve two rites of passage: attaining a driver's license, and having a car of one's own. For some, owning a particular make or model of car was important; for others, a statement of individuality could be made with a personalized license plate or a bumper sticker. But for the car customizer, the need to transform through rebuilding, decorating and naming was far more vital. A kustom car is not a car for all seasons, however. "Sometimes", said one observer, "they sit more than they go," but when the kustom cars are on the road, it's a great day. From their shiny exteriors to their glistening interiors, each is a triumph over time and a tribute to the skills and energies of its owner.

5 - The Chivas of Colombia

Partygoers, politicians, newlyweds and tourists all ride Colombia's chivas, as do country people and city folk with all of their belongings and animals. Chivas are the most practical way to travel, say aficionados of the gaily painted wooden trucks, as there always seems to be room for just one more person or package. Most Colombians refer to these vehicles as "chivas", except in the Nariño area where they are known as "guaguas" and in the Antioquia area where "camion de escalera" (ladder truck) is the accepted term. Chivas were once found throughout the country, but today they are mainly driven in the valley of the Cauca river, along the Caribbean coast (in Barranquilla and Cartagena) and in Antioquia. Chi-

vas often provide the only transportation service to rural communities. They transport cargo and passengers to the larger cities, but seldom run regular routes in urban areas where metal-bodied buses have replaced them.

Chivas, camiones de escalera and guaguas vary in their names, decoration and geographic origins. All are painted, wooden-bodied vehicles. But, due to climate, some vehicles are built with openings to capture the slightest breeze, while others are enclosed to a greater degree to keep their passengers dry and warm. The trucks begin with a Ford, Dodge or Chevrolet engine and cab. Contractors then build a complete wooden superstructure starting from the cab and extending over the rear axle, just as the Haitian carpenters do for their larger size Tap-Taps. The length of the chiva is conceived in terms of its removable benches. It can be a 4, 5, 7, or 9 bench chiva. The left or driver's side of the vehicle is closed, with inset windows; the right side is left open to allow passengers to enter every row or bench of seats. Passengers riding on the roof hold on to a railing built around the entire top. A rear panel on the body can be lowered to support additional freight, and one or more benches can be removed to hold still more cargo. Metal panels are often nailed over the wooden superstructure for greater durability. Chivas usually have windows in back and along the closed side, with oilcloth curtains available on the open side to protect passengers from inclement weather.

Chivas with their one side open, one side closed arrangement resemble the open car design of electric trolleys popular in the United States between the 1880's and the First World War. The open trolley car had similar transverse benches across its entire width and longitudinal steps (as does the chiva) for entering and leaving the vehicle. The railing enclosing the chiva's roof is

The space between the hood and the driver's door is large enough for a multicolored geometric design.

A camion de escalera in
Cocorna. Photograph
courtesy of Camilo
Moreno.

A venerable four bench camion de escalera built on a 1933 Ford body. Photographed in Cartago by Camilo Moreno.

somewhat echoed by the rooftop of the electric trolley which concealed the electrical connection to the trolley wires above the street.

According to Genevieve Bellis, who lived in Bogota just after the Second World War, open and closed electric trolleys carried passengers in the Colombian capitol at that time. Bellis mentioned both the open trolley car with its benches and a closed, seatless trolley which carried "a motley assortment of cargo" and passengers who rode standing up. These trolleys were city-operated, but Bogota also had privately owned buses at the time, which were "thrown together locally" and were often quite dilapidated. By the 1960's as an

English writer Glynis Anthony noted, the private company buses were "boldly painted with all forms of traffic art emblazoned on their sides." Today, Bogota's buses are built of metal, have closed sides and are painted with geometric designs. There is much variety in the colors and shapes decorating the hoods, sides and bumpers of these buses, but the figurative art which Mrs. Anthony had seen two decades earlier has now disappeared from Bogota's buses.

Chivas are built in workshops (talleres) much like those of the Tap-Tap contractors in Haiti. Miguel Plabon, whose taller is in Itagui, near Medellin, said his crew completes approximate-

Additional complex abstractions appear on the side of each bench or row of seats.

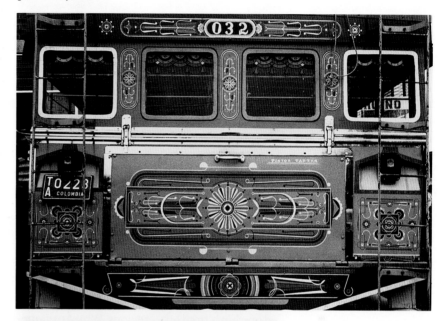

Even the tasseled curtains are reduced to semicircles in this symphony of circles and squares painted by Tarzan.

Jorge Betancour or "Tarzan" painting the letters of the company name on a camion de escalera at the Taller Baru.

ly ten new chivas each year. Depending on the number of workers involved on each job, a new chiva could take from two weeks to a month to complete, at a cost of approximately $2,800.00 for construction and painting. At Dario Blandon's Taller Baru, in Medellin, there were eight chivas being painted, built, or repaired during a recent visit. Other chiva workshops exist in small towns wherever these vehicles are found.

Chivas are painted in styles which vary according to the region of the country. For many

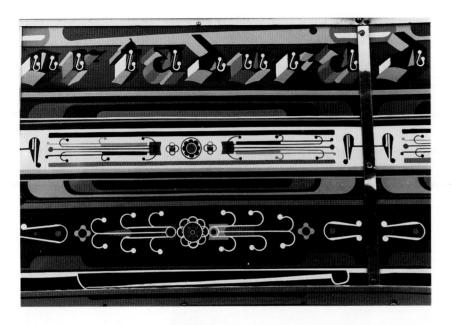

Deciphering the name of the company becomes difficult once the letters are shaded.

ments drawn first with pencil and ruler, then painted with a brush fastened into one arm of a compass. The name of the bus company or owner is lettered just below the window area on the closed side of the vehicle. Each letter is treated as if carved in relief, but the perspective portion is rainbow-hued so that a blue letter "A", for example, will grow a yellow, green or pink shadow to extend its solidity. Letters and shapes are usually the only designs seen on the sides of these vehicles. Any figurative painting is reserved for the back panel, precisely as is done in Panama and Haiti.

The back of a camion de escalera is divided into a band of windows, a central area for the painting, and a "frame" created by the ladders attached to the vehicle body to enable passengers to climb to the roof with their cargo. The back windows may be decorated with the name of the route (such as "Medellin - Bello") and with suggestions of flowers or tied-back curtains. One vehicle being painted in the Plabon Taller had a place name on each window with a landscape evocative of the place painted below it.

Around and near the rear tail lights, license plate and bumper there is also space for other designs. In the back center panel is the artist's principal painting. The subject matter for such painting may be religious, pastoral, humorous, or even suggestive of changes in the modern world. The same religious lithographs which were used for vehicular art in Panama and in Haiti also serve as an inspiration for paintings in Colombia. These lithographs and resulting paintings include the Passion of Christ, the Life of the Virgin, or events in the lives of the saints. "El Senor Caido" (Christ, seen falling under the weight of the cross) is a frequent subject because of its connection with the nearby pilgrimage site at Girardota, a small town located twenty six kilom-

Colombians, the camiones de escalera of Antioquia are the most beautiful. The complicated geometric patterns and the rear panel paintings are far more elaborate than anything normally painted on chivas from other regions. Why Antioqueno painters have developed such a tradition is unclear, but few camiones de escalera in use seem to lack the characteristic rear panel painting and side details. One explanation was offered in an article written by Dario Ruiz Gomez. He argues that the craft tradition in the Province of Antioquia could be dated to the establishment of a vocational art school in Medellin in 1867. Respect for materials was taught along with knowledge of artistic trends. Thus, when contractors began building camiones de escalera the region already had a heritage of many decades of practical art education.

Along both sides of the camion de escalera are carefully measured and spaced geometric ele-

Town names with appropriate scenes are noted on a camion de escalera being completed at the Taller Plabon. The jet in the Rionegro panel represents Medellin's airport.

El Señor Caido (the Fallen Christ) is seen in this version painted by Julio C. Florez.

Hernando Perez's panel of the Virgin and Child was probably inspired by a lithograph.

eters from Medellin. Landscapes may be as generic as a cottage by a lake or as specific as the Golden Gate bridge. Miguel Plabon keeps on hand several examples of scenic postal cards which he had used as sources for camion de escalera paintings, transferring these images to the panels with a grid system.

Postal card views may have provided the inspiration for other panel paintings as well. In the catalogue of a 1986 exhibition of vehicular art, held in Medellin at the Banco de la Republica, one camion de escalera painting was based on the 1857 painting called "The Gleaners" by Jean Francois Millet. Although the flat plains of France are very different from the mountainous terrain of Colombia, still the hardworking peasants portrayed by Millet could easily be understood by Colombian campesinos.

The subject for a camion de escalera panel painting is selected by the owner or the driver. It reflects his taste and that of the rural community from which his business is derived. The more urban choices of film and music stars, as seen on vehicles in Panama and Haiti, are not repeated in Colombia. In fact, no paintings of living individuals were seen at all, although the portraits of both Che Guevara and Pope John Paul II are supposed to grace some camion de escalera

An unsigned view of a California bridge is noted on a camion de escalera photographed in La Ceja.

A postal card view may
have been the source for
this view of a mountain
lake.

Worthy of Utrillo is this view of a local church.

P. Arnulfo Villa's little boy has teased the dog once too often on "El Chico", a camion de escalera photographed in Guarne.

Tarzan meets a tiger in this detail of a panel scene by H. Moncada. Photograph courtesy of Camilo Moreno.

panels. Camilo Moreno, photographer, and curator of the exhibition at the Banco de la Republica, said that while some artists tended to repeat basic types of paintings, others experiment with new subject matter. One such artist, Jorge Betancour, signs his work as "Tarzan" or "Pintor Tarzan". Tarzan has done landscapes, comic episodes, a series of jungle animals and even jet airplanes. Tarzan, according to Camilo Moreno, is interested in new themes for vehicular painting, and will continue to vary his work in the future.

Camion de escalera painters serve apprenticeships in the workshops of the various contractors. It is often a family affair with sons learning the skills from their fathers, as did Miguel Plabon, who began his now fifty-year long career as a teenager. About a dozen men are currently active as camion de escalera painters in the Medellin area. Of that group, Tarzan and Albeiro Tamayo are often mentioned as the most talented. Julio C. Florez, who was featured in an explanatory video tape made for the Banco de la Republica exhibit, is one of several older masters who have died recently.

Red, yellow and green, the colors of the Colombian flag, are used to designate the routes followed by the camiones de escalera. Red vehicles go north to the mining areas and towns such

An old lion
yawns in a
panel
photographed
in Rionegro.

Storytelling panels are popular, as in this study of billiard playing dogs painted by Tarzan. Photographed in Rionegro.

A camion de escalera
loaded with produce
which came from Andes
to the Playa Mayorista
market in Medellin.

as Remedios and Zaragoza. Yellow vehicles head
east to Rionegro and Marinilla. Green vehicles
travel on the coffee roads to Caldas, while blue
vehicles are bound for Bolivar, Andes and Jardin.
Red, yellow, blue, green, white and black are the
basic colors of a painter's palette, although he
may add other shades for his major rear panel
efforts.

Each camion de escalera has its driver and
his agile assistant. Called a "fogonero" (or fireman,
a term derived from railroading), the assistant's
job is to load the vehicle and collect the fares. Ob-
servers are often impressed with the fogonero's
ability to load expeditiously and to recall exactly

whose parcel is where. But, as a driver once told
me when I was travelling with a chicken on his
bus in Africa, "Woman, mark your fowl!" so quite
probably riders learn to mark their fowls and other cargo as well.

What is the future of the chiva? Will it soon
be replaced by metal buses everywhere, just as
has been the case in some of the larger Colombian cities? For lovers of vehicular art, the answer
is that chivas will probably be on the road for at
least a while longer. The development of transportation in Colombia has been described as leap-
ing rapidly from the mule to the airplane. Due
to the geography of the country it was easier to

There is plenty of room remaining on the roof of "El Jigante", a camion de escalera photographed by Camilo Moreno.

walk or use the rivers than to build roads or railroads. Colombia was the first country in Latin America to have a functioning airline (established in 1920) so travel by air had developed faster than by land. Although Colombia is said to have 700 airports, there are still many persons in rural places who depend on their local chiva service. Camilo Moreno points out that the chivas provide a vital economic link. Country people travel to town with their produce and return home with commodities from the city. Such travel would be too expensive for the average campesino to do by airplane even if he lived near one of the many airports.

The chiva serves as basic transport, but it has other functions as well. Suitably decorated chivas attend weddings and funerals. Politicians campaign in them and include chivas as national symbols in televised "get out the vote" commercials. Hotels in several large cities have purchased chivas to take tourists on evening sightseeing tours. Miguel Plabon said that he was building tourist chivas for cities throughout Colombia. These smaller bodied chivas, often using Toyota cabs and engines, are already in use in Medellin and San Andres. An advertisement in a Cali newspaper invited visitors to enjoy their city by riding in a chiva, so presumably many future tourists will also be able to enjoy their sightseeing Colombian style.

Beautiful flowers were used to make this camion de escalera ready for a wedding in Cali. Photograph courtesy of Camilo Moreno.

Geometric forms assembled to suggest a rocket ship are found on the back of the mirror. Photograph courtesy of Dicken Castro.

special destination chivas carries its assortment of appropriately dressed clay passengers and, as one writer expressed it, "a load of packages and legends". The Vargas chivas are widely sold in Colombia and abroad.

A painter born in Antioquia, Gabriel Jaime Sencial, has exhibited both paintings and assemblages inspired by the art of the chiva. Sencial's "back-of-the-truck" views incorporate the ladders, windows, license plate, taillights and painted landscapes seen on a typical camion de escalera. Critics have compared his works to the "readymades" of Marcel Duchamp in their use of authentic materials.

Chivas are painted with both geometric designs and realistic imagery derived from a number of sources. Colombian architect and graphic designer Dicken Castro had studied the shapes and colors used by chiva painters. He has written that the shapes themselves are similar in some ways to the Art Deco designs of the 1930's, but have now evolved into an entire visual vocabulary. Castro has in fact created various works using this symbolic language. One series of sixteen prints was completed for the First Salon Op of Graphic Design, held in Bogota in 1983. Visitors to the exhibition could rearrange the set of prints in innumerable combinations in much the same way that chiva painters do with compass and ruler. Castro feels that these forms offer an important basis for a unique national art style. Castro has also used the block letters of chiva names in some of his serigraphs.

In addition to exhibitions featuring the works of artists inspired by chiva forms and symbols there have been at least two displays of the art of these Colombian vehicles. The 1986 exhibit held at the Banco de la Republica in Medellin was accompanied by a full color catalogue and three video tape films dealing with the painters and the

Like the Tap-Tap and ox cart, the chiva is an important part of Colombian art and popular traditions. Tales are told, songs are sung, and models are made of these vehicles. They are part of folklore and art as both symbol and subject. Clay chivas in various sizes, for example, are the specialty of a potter living in Pitalito, near Huila. Cecilia Vargas' mother was a well-known maker of clay figurines. Cecilia followed the tradition of making small sculptures, but changed the format. Rather than making freestanding figures by hand or in molds, she made clay people who rode in chivas decorated for weddings, funerals, or for trips to relax by the river. Each of these small, vehicles. A competition in Cali in 1985 sought to determine the most beautiful chiva, certainly not an easy task.

The chiva, like the other painted vehicles considered in this book, is an important form of popular culture in its native land. Its decoration, according to Cecilia Duque, director of the Museo de Artes y Tradiciones Populares in Bogota, shows creativity even when the artists copy from other media. As Gerard Alexis, director of the Musee National in Port-au-Prince, said of the Tap-Taps of his country, "It is an art of the unnecessary; the decoration does not make them go faster or better". Needed or not, the decorations on these vehicles offer their owners and painters the means and a very visible location for self-expression. It has been said that naming a vehicle is an almost universal tendency. The owners of the vehicles in this book have often named them, as well as decorated them. Their achievements enrich all our lives as we view the passing traffic carrying "Art on the Road."

The vehicle itself poses for its portrait. Photograph courtesy of Camilo Moreno.

Afterword and Acknowledgments

Art on the Road has been underway for almost ten years. It began in 1977 during a family trip to Colombia. While wandering through the old city of Cartagena, we spotted a truly ferocious truck, our first Colombian chiva. This chiva had jagged painted teeth along the edges of its fenders. It looked ready to eat up the miles and probably the highway as well. But despite our fascination with this "Jaws" of transportation, the first has become the last; we began the research for this book in Costa Rica, saving Colombia for the grand finale.

In each country we visited we were fortunate enough to find helpful and knowledgable sources. There was not always a great deal of information in print, but many people knew where to find the artists, their workshops and, above all, the vehicles. We have quoted many of the people we interviewed in the chapters dealing with their country's painted vehicles, but we would also like to thank those who have helped us to discover the history and development of the carreta, chiva, Tap-Tap, bus, and car. We would like especially to thank members of the Chaverri and Alfaro families of Sarchi, Costa Rica, and Don Carlos Balser and Don Enrique Vargas, both of San Jose, Costa Rica. In Panama City, Nelson Romero, Norma Salazar, Francisco Robles, Monica Kupfer, Sandra Eleta, and Jesus Teodoro de Villarue gave us appreciated assistance. In Haiti we learned about Tap-Taps from Gerald Alexis, Francine Murat, Rodney Flambert and Mario Arnault. Insights and information on the world of kustom cars came from Steve Anderson, Dale Laroche, Butch Swanson, Dave Bell, Jerry Thomson, Jon Kosmoski, Patrick Lehman, and M. K. John. For the chivas of Colombia, we are grateful for the help of Antonio Grass, Alberto Riviera Gutierrez, Cecelia Duque Duque, Dicken Castro, Camilo Moreno and Marta Leonor Davila.

We appreciate, finally, the guidance generously offered by Robert Farris Thompson, Ute Stebich, Harold E. Hinds, Jr. and Bernard Guillaume. Research is sometimes a lonely endeavor. That was not the case with *Art on the Road*. Everywhere people were generous in sharing their knowledge and insights. We hope that we have repaid these kindnesses by demonstrating in words and pictures some of the delightful examples of travelling art we have seen. As a spectator at a local car show said, very appreciatively, "That's a really mean car". And, they were all just that.

Further Reading

Ox Carts of Costa Rica:

John and Mavis Biesanz. COSTA RICAN LIFE. New York: Columbia University Press, 1944.

Frederick Boyle. A RIDE ACROSS A CONTINENT. A PERSONAL NARRATIVE OF WANDERINGS THROUGH NICARAGUA AND COSTA RICA. London: Richard Bentley. 2 vols., 1868.

R. Fernandez Guardia, ed. COSTA RICA EN EL SIGLO XIX. ANTOLOGIA DE VIAJEROS. San Jose: Editorial Universitaria Centroamericana. 3rd. edit., 1972.

Constantino Lascaris and Guillermo Malavassi. LA CARRETA COSTARRICENSE. San Jose: Editorial Costa Rica, 3rd edit., 1985.

Luis Marden. "Land of the Painted Oxcarts", NATIONAL GEOGRAPHIC MAGAZINE, XC: 4, October, 1946, 409-456.

August Panyella, ed. FOLK ART OF THE AMERICAS. New York: Harry N. Abrams, 1981.

Alberto Quijano Quesada. COSTA RICA AYER Y HOY. San Jose: Editorial Borrase Hermanos, 1939.

Robert de Roos. "Costa Rica. Free of the Volcano's Veil", NATIONAL GEOGRAPHIC MAGAZINE, 128: l, January, 1965, 125–152.

Anthony Trollope. THE WEST INDIES AND THE SPANISH MAIN. London: Chapman and Hall, 1860.

John Lloyd Stephens. INCIDENTS OF TRAVEL IN CENTRAL AMERICA, CHIAPAS AND YUCATAN. New York: Dover Publications, 1969. [First edition published in New York, 1841].

Mary Louise Wilkinson. "The Colorful Carts of Sarchi", AMERICAS, 38: 3, May-June, 1986, 8-13.

Buses of Panama:

Julio Arosemena M. "Algunas consideraciones sobre los rotulos y las pinturas en los medios de transporte de la ciudad de Panama (Un tema de folklore urbano)", LOTERIA, 1974, 11-43.

Karen Asis. "Paint your Wagon", TRAVEL - HOLIDAY, February, 1986, 92.

Peter S. Briggs, "Panamanian Popular Art from the Back of a Bus", STUDIES IN LATIN AMERICAN POPULAR CULTURE, l, 1982, 187-195.

Charles E. Cobb, Jr. "Panama: Ever at the Crossroads", NATIONAL GEOGRAPHIC MAGAZINE, 169:4, April, 1986, 466-492.

Gloria Fraser Giffords. "Soul of the Mexican Trucker", EL PALACIO, 87:1, Spring, 1981, 3-17.

Maureen Hillpot. "A Canvas of Panama", TAXI, 2:7, July, 1987, 140-153.

Harold E. Hinds, Jr. "Kaliman: Mexico's Most Popular Superhero", STUDIES IN LATIN AMERICAN POPULAR CULTURE, 4, 1985, 27-42.

James R. Jaquith. "Cawboy de Medianoche", THE NEW SCHOLAR, 5:l, 1975, 39-72.

Silvano Lora. "La Pintura Popular en Panama", LOTERIA, #208, 1973, 109-124.

Ramon Oviero. "La Pintura en los buses: un arte popular", LA PRENSA, August 26, 1983.

Mary Louise Wilkinson. "Panama's Moving Murals", AMERICAS, 39:2, March - April, 1987, 44-47.

——, "Homenaje a un Arte Popular: Los Buses de Panama". Panama City: Museo de Arte Contemporaneo, 1983. (Exhibition Catalogue).

Tap-Taps of Haiti:

Gerald Alexis, Jeanine Liautaud, Michele Celestin, Sabine Mallebranche, Pascale Wagner. "Art et Culture: Le Tour de la Question: Les Taps Taps", LE NOUVELLISTE, Port-au-Prince, Septembre-Octobre, 1985.

Tracy Atkinson. HAITI: THE NAIVE TRADITION. THE FLAGG TANNING CORPORATION COLLECTION. Milwaukee: Milwaukee Art Center, 1974. (Exhibition Catalogue).

Le Grace Benson. "A Report from Haiti", ART INTERNATIONAL, XXVI: 5-6, May-June, 1982, 117-130.

Hugh B. Cave. HAITI. HIGHROAD TO ADVENTURE. New York: Henry Holt and Co., 1952.

Georges Corvington. PORT-AU-PRINCE AU COURS DES ANS. Volumes: "La Metropole Haitienne due XIXe siecle 1888-1915" and "La capital d'Haiti sous l'Occupation 1915-22". Port-au-Prince: Imprimerie Henri Deschamps, 1984.

Wade Davis. THE SERPENT AND THE RAINBOW. New York: Simon and Schuster, 1985.

Carole Devillers. "Haiti's Voodoo Pilgrimages of Spirits and Saints", NATIONAL GEOGRAPHIC MAGAZINE, 167:3 March, 1985, 395-408

Clyde H. Farnsworth. "Haiti's Artists Hurting as Tourist Trade Falls", THE NEW YORK TIMES, June 13, 1984.

June E. Hahner. "Brazilian Truck Bumper Sayings", REVISTA INTERAMERICANA, V: 3, Fall, 1975, 422-432.

L. G. Hoffman. HAITIAN ART. THE LEGEND AND LEGACY OF THE NAIVE TRADITION. Davenport: Davenport Art Gallery, 1985. (Exhibition Catalogue).

James S. Kus. "Peruvian Religious Truck Names", NAMES, 27:3, September, 1979, 179-187.

Alfred Metraux, VOODOO IN HAITI. New York: Oxford University Press, 1959.

Seldon Rodman. THE MIRACLE OF HAITIAN ART. Garden City: Doubleday and Company, 1974.

Ute Stebich. HAITIAN ART. Brooklyn: The Brooklyn Museum, 1978. (Exhibition Catalogue).

Edna Taft. A PURITAN IN VOODOO-LAND. Philadelphia: The Penn Publishing Company, 1938.

Robert Farris Thompson. FLASH OF THE SPIRIT. AFRICAN AND AFRO-AMERICAN ART AND PHILOSOPHY. New York: Random House, 1983.

Robert Farris Thompson and Joseph Cornet. THE FOUR MOMENTS OF THE SUN. KONGO ART IN TWO WORLDS. Washington, D. C.: National Gallery of Art, 1981. (Exhibition Catalogue).

Kustom Cars of the United States

Frances Basham, Bob Ughetti and Paul Ramboli. CAR CULTURE. New York: Delilah Communications, Ltd. 1984.

Peggy V. Beck. "The Low Riders. Folk Art and Emergent Nationalism". NATIVE ARTS/ WEST, 1:4, October, 1980, 25-27.

Colin Burnham. CUSTOMIZING CARS. New York: Arco Publishing, Inc., 1984 (2d ed).

James R. Chiles. "The Great American Junkyard: going from wrecks to riches", SMITHSONIAN, 15:12, March, 1985, 52-63.

Cynthia Golomb Dettelbach. IN THE DRIVER'S SEAT: A STUDY OF THE AUTOMOBILE IN AMERICAN LITERATURE AND POPULAR CULTURE. Westport, Ct: Greenwood Press, 1976.

Jay Hirsch. GREAT AMERICAN DREAM MACHINES: Classic Cars of the 50s and 60s. New York: Macmillan Publishing Company, 1985.

Mike Key. LEAD SLEDS. London: Osprey Publishing Ltd., 1984.

Beverly Rae Kimes, ed. THE AMERICAN CAR SINCE 1775. New York: Dutton, 1971.

Peter Marsh and Peter Collett. "Driving Passion", PSYCHOLOGY TODAY. June, 1987, 16-24.

Andrew Morland. STREET RODS. London: Osprey Publishing, Ltd. 1983.

Phil Patton. OPEN ROAD. A Celebration of the American Highway. New York: Simon & Schuster, Inc., 1987.

Jim Potter and George Barris. CUSTOM CARS 1957 ANNUAL. Los Angeles: Trend Books, 1956.

Kirk L. Ready. CUSTOM CARS. Minneapolis: Lerner Publications, 1982.

Gerald Silk, Angelo Tito Anselmi, Strother MacMinn and Henry Flood Robert, Jr. AUTOMOBILE AND CULTURE. New York: Harry N. Abrams, Inc. 1984 (Exhibition Catalogue).

Bill Sumner. "In the Eye of the Beholder. The Consecrated Cars of the Bhagwan", AUTOMOBILE QUARTERLY, XXIV: 4, 1986, 394-403.

Paul C. Wilson. CHROME DREAMS. Automobile Styling since 1893. Radnor, PA.: Chilton Book Company, 1976.

Tom Wolfe. THE KANDY*COLORED TANGERINE*FLAKE STREAMLINE BABY. New York: Pocket Book, 1966 (1st ed., 1965).

Tom Wolfe. THE PUMP HOUSE GANG. New York: Farrar, Straus & Giroux, 1968.

—— THE BEST OF HOT ROD MAGAZINE. Los Angeles: Petersen Publishing Co., 1986.

Chivas of Colombia:

Glynis Anthony. COLOMBIA: LAND OF TOMORROW. London: Robert Hale, 1968.

Claudine Bancelin. "No me bajo de este bus", REVISTA AVIANCA, 87, 114-118.

Genevieve Hoehn Bellis. TEN ROOMS AND TWO PATIOS. Harrisburg: The Evangelical Press, 1948.

Alvaro Gartner. "Las Chivas: puro folclor rodante", LA PATRIA, April 8, 1983.

Dario Ruiz Gomez. "El camion de escalera", REVISTA LAMPARA, XXIV: 100, Junio 1986, 23-9.

Sonia Gonzalez de Vengoechea. "Chivas cargadas de bultos y leyendas", EL TIEMPO, April 13, 1985.

Gertrude Litto. SOUTH AMERICAN FOLK POTTERY. New York: Watson-Guptill Publications, 1976.

Camilo Moreno. "Que Chiva!" EL MUNDO (Medellin), Mayo 12, 1985.

Patrick Rouillard. ANTIOQUIA. Medellin: Editorial Colina, 1985 (2d Ed.).

——— "Los Camiones de Escalera". Medellin: Banco de la Republica, 1986 (Exhibition Catalogue).